THE COSMO-BIOGRAPHY OF SUNRA

The Sound of Joy Is Enlightening

Chris Raschka

CANDLEWICK PRESS

For Paul and Renate — musical mentors

[S]un Ra always said that he came from Saturn.

Now, you know and I know that this is silly. No one comes from Saturn.

And yet.

If he did come from Saturn, it would explain so much.

Let's say he did come from Saturn.

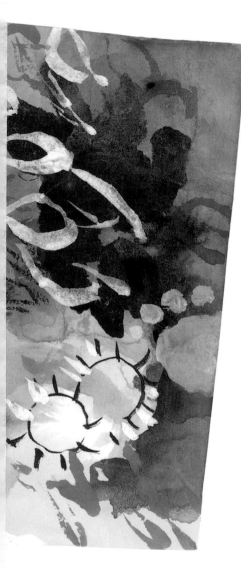

Well, on May 22, 1914, Sun Ra landed on Earth.

Looking around, he found himself in Birmingham, Alabama.
His parents named him Herman and called him Sonny.

Being from another planet, Sun Ra was naturally interested in everything earthy. Trees, clouds, and spotted dogs; apples, hot dogs, and corn on the cob; hats, socks, and wigs; drawing, dancing, and throwing a ball.

And most of all, music!

It was the thing about the earth that was most like the stars.

It is not so surprising that Sun Ra was a musical genius. He was a fine piano player by the time he was eleven. He could notate music that he heard on the radio or in dance halls.

Sun Ra noticed the books in the library of the black Masonic Temple and he spent many hours reading about the great philosophies of the earth, including Rosicrucianism and Freemasonry (which another musical genius, Mozart, had also been curious about).

One thing puzzled Sun Ra. The earthlings insisted on sorting themselves into two varieties: the white variety and the black variety. Sun Ra was sorted into the black variety.

Also, the name his parents had given him, Herman Blount, hardly seemed the name of someone from Saturn. As soon as he could, Sun Ra changed his name to Le Sony'r Ra, and then simply to Sun Ra.

As a teen earthling, Sun Ra spent long afternoons at the Forbes Piano Company, where, even though the store was owned by earthlings of the white variety, he was welcome to play, compose, or just practice the piano.

Before he left high school, Sun Ra was already a professional musician, leading his own ensemble and accompanying singers.

hen Sun Ra saw the strangest thing. All over the globe, the earthlings began fighting and killing each other. It was the Second World War.

Sun Ra refused to join in.

Questioning him, the Birmingham draft board understood that his conscience would not allow him to fight (little did they know that he was from Saturn!), so they designated him a conscientious objector. Instead of going to war, Sun Ra was sent to work in a forest in Pennsylvania.

After the war, wishing to learn more about earthly music, Sun Ra traveled to Chicago to absorb its blues, doo-wop, and jazz. Sun Ra mastered all of these, both as a performer and a composer.

Julian Priester

Pat Patrick

John Thompson

John Gilmore

Sun Ra drew other musicians to him. They played in small groups, medium-size groups, and big groups, with singers or without singers — all kinds of ways. They were like sailors on a boat bound for a new world, a new world of sound.

And like all good sailors, they played and danced and sang while their captain, Sun Ra, steered the ship. They called themselves the Arkestra.

moog iii

Being from outer space, Sun Ra was afraid neither of electrons nor electricity and so was one of the first musicians on Earth to use an electric keyboard. He played the Mini-Moog, the Clavinet, and the Rock-Si-Chord.

clavinet

Rock-Si-Chord

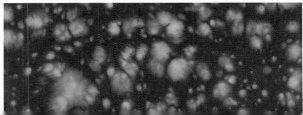

Between working at night and rehearsals in the morning, Sun Ra browsed in Chicago's bookstores or spent the long afternoons simply walking the city's streets and avenues. He was an intergalactic boulevardier.

This left little time for sleeping. In his life on Earth, Sun Ra rarely slept for several hours in a bed.

He took short naps throughout the day,
sometimes even dozing during his own
rehearsals. When he woke again,
he immediately continued with what
he had just been doing.

In the early 1960s, Sun Ra sailed with the Arkestra to New York City.

Though some New Yorkers complained that Sun Ra was *too far out* (what did they expect from a Saturnian?), the wise ones, like Dizzy Gillespie and Thelonious Monk, said,

"Keep it up, Sonny," and *"Yeah . . . it swings!"*

Ronnie Boykins

Marshall Allen

June Tyson

Would it surprise you that the Arkestra made its own clothes? Robes of purple cotton, silk scarves, bone necklaces, and crowns of shining metal foil.

From this time on, joining the Arkestra meant being ready to live with the Arkestra, rehearse with the Arkestra, and perform with the Arkestra, sometimes playing for many, many hours on end.

The music might be crisp and tight one moment, then wild and free the next, changing with a nod of Sun Ra's head or a wave of his fingers.

One disadvantage of coming from Saturn, though, was that Sun Ra could never really understand or care too much about money.

The New York landlords, on the other hand, did, and kicked the Arkestra out, so they sailed again, this time to Philadelphia, renting a house there.

With Philadelphia as their home port, the Arkestra traveled all around the earth, playing, singing, and dancing for people who spoke every language.

Of all the places they visited, Sun Ra's favorite was where the Great Pyramids stand in the sands of Egypt.

At last, after seventy-nine years, it was time for Sun Ra to say good-bye to the earth and all his friends there. On May 30, 1993, he returned to Saturn.

Before he left, Sun Ra said, "You may think that it is gravity that holds us all together but it is not—it is music."

Sun Ra, who was born in 1914 in Alabama with the name Herman P. "Sonny" Blount, became a pianist, a composer, a conductor, a teacher, a businessman, and a poet. For most of the twentieth century, Sun Ra made music that is still hard to define, perhaps because he loved all music, from the poppiest pop to the weightiest classic. Always, he created his life and his music his own way, even unto the fabulous robes he and his orchestra, the Arkestra, wore when they performed. Choosing to forgo the traditional route of signing with a record label, Sun Ra released nearly all of his music independently.

Selected Recordings:

Sun Song (1956)

Super-Sonic Jazz (1956)

Sound of Joy (1957)

Visits Planet Earth (1958)

Jazz in Silhouette (1959)

Sound Sun Pleasure!! (1960)

Interstellar Low Ways (1960)

The Futuristic Sounds of Sun Ra (1961)

We Travel the Spaceways (1961)

Other Planes of There (1964)

The Magic City (1965)

The Heliocentric Worlds of Sun Ra, Vols. 1 and 2 (1965)

Monorails and Satellites (1966)

Nothing Is (1966)

Outer Spaceways Incorporated (1968)

Atlantis (1969)

My Brother the Wind, Vol. 2 (1970)

Universe in Blue (1972)

Space Is the Place (1972)

Lanquidity (1978)

The Antique Blacks (1978)

Sleeping Beauty (1979)

On Jupiter (1979)

Sun Ra Arkestra Meets Salah Ragab in Egypt (1984)

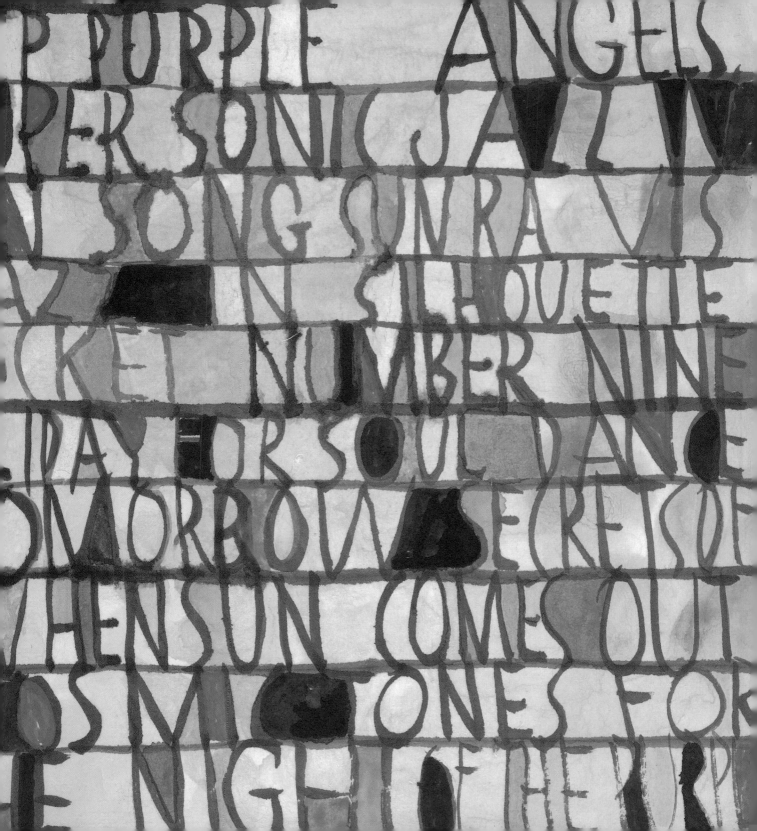